UNBROKEN & EXPOSED

WELCOME HOME

Janelle Marie Comstock

BookLeaf Publishing

India | USA | UK

Made with ❤ on the BookLeaf Publishing Platform

www.bookleafpub.in

www.bookleafpub.com

Dedication

To my friends who have inspired me and shared their authenticity and vulnerability; you are courageous; from this I have drawn my own strength to share myself with you.

Preface

My name is Janelle Marie Comstock. It is my pleasure to share with you my first ever, and hopefully not my last, book of poetry woven with some of my favorite genres of fantasy, creativity, spirituality, personal life experiences, and favorite moments with special people. I was inspired by a friend (RICH) who introduced me to a local open mic night through a group called WORDISM, and I experienced the creativity of many writers. Having a dream to be an author when I was in fourth grade, I am finally unleashing my imagination as an outlet for creative expression. As a therapist, it is an honor to have a tool that I can use for myself while also encouraging others to use writing as a support on their mental health journey. I hope you have as much fun reading my poetry as I did creating it! Enjoy!

Acknowledgements

For my beautiful children, your birth stories are precious and thus a center of this book, you are *ALL* my *EVERYTHING*.

1. A Life Chosen

I reflect on the winding paths
that I've taken.
I lie on the floor, my heart nearly
breaking.
This journey has been
remarkably challenging.
Feeling uneven, off-kilter,
wobbly, balancing.
Has this path been a lie? All an
illusion?
"Oh no, my dear girl," (a
whispered delusion?)

Disenchanted memories flash
through my mind.
"This lesson will lead you to more
like your kind."
A journey of heart and soul and
divine spirit.
My guides susurration, "I can
finally hear it!"
The anguish bleeds out, "Is there
a resolution?"
"Was I an experiment, a forlorn
conclusion?"
I hear another whisper...
"You chose this life, this anguish,
this precise path."
And suddenly I realize... this...

is... my soul contract.

2. Reflection

A newborn baby arrives, perfect
and pink.
On a beautiful, frigid, afternoon
of the twenty-fifth.
The angels whisper, "Cherish this
moment...don't blink."
She is special, unique, a force to
reckon with.
Dark hair, hazel eyes, and lips
pursed and puckered.
Her beauty within will soon be
uncovered.

Her locks soon fall out, revealing
strawberry blonde.
A mother's love, an unwavering
bond.
She snuggles close to her mother
to breastfeed.
This moment of innocence;
beauty indeed.
Frozen in time with amazement
and wonder.
A miraculous moment between
child and mother.
Tender moments, tiny toes, a
squinted nose.
You are my beautiful, perfect,
April Rose.

3. Angelic

The cry echoes throughout the
maternity ward.
Carefully cut is the umbilical
cord.
A new life, an old soul, enters
this world.
From Spirit to Earth this infant is
whirled.
An infant so fierce, yet so soft,
and so tender.
No need to conform to Earthly
pressure.

A sweet baby boy, with love like
no other.
Unconditional love flows from
his mother.
Soon smiles and giggles follow
with time.
You love to dance, to play cars,
and make sticky slime.
The bliss of a healthy,
imaginative boy.
It is a treasure to see your eyes
twinkle with joy.
A gentle baby boy, a mother
smitten.
I love you son, angelic, Andrew
Christian.

4. Miracle

Awakened suddenly by pains and
a dream.
A mother with child, "Too early,"
I screamed.
Rushed to the hospital, weary
with fear.
Is the baby breathing, I gasp
through the tears.
Concerned faces glance all
around the room.
My heart throbs, I feel the energy
of doom.

Then suddenly, a gentle hand, a
nurse.
"She is alright," comforting, yet
terse.
Whisked away to the NICU, she
is gone with such haste.
Alone, dazed, and confused,
written all over my face.
Hours pass by, I'm finally able to
see her.
A relief, she is safe...a day of blur.
Kaitlyn Elizabeth, I watch you
breathe through a spiracle.
You are nothing short of a
wonderous miracle.

5. Awakened

I was always so practical, and so
grounded.
Never believed in the, "Woo,
Woo," with judgement clouded.
Til one day, I opened my mind
and my heart.
I felt transformations like being
pierced with a dart.
Once open to more, I was in awe
to my soul.
An entirely new world, to
become truly whole.

I felt a presence of others so true.
A genuine fire, kindled life anew.
"Where do I begin or go from here?"
With wonder I am drawn to more, without fear.
My journey begins now, I am awakened.
My guides lead the way now, my spirit engravened.
I live with more liveliness, more purpose, more wisdom.
Sharing myself and my gifts with intention and vision.

6. Mya

A little dachshund pup one year
old.
You are so sweet and squiggly to
hold.
Our first family pup, bringing joy
to our children.
Our hearts bursting with eternal
love, tenderly smitten.
The kids have more excitement
than me!
How can that possibly be?
You follow me around the house

to every room.

Waiting under my feet, almost

stepping on you, VROOM!

You are faithful, love rides, walks,

and belly rubs.

One time you chased something

under the porch and through the

shrubs.

With beautiful long ears, you

love to eat chicken and meat.

A cunning pup with a heart so

sweet!

Mya, "The Nose," you are loved

and missed.

Know that we have always

cherished you; you are
sunkissed!

7. Ellie

Oh, my beautiful pup of 2020.

In a world so uncertain, in chaos
and frenzy.

In many ways, crumbling, falling
apart.

And there you were, a missing
piece of my heart.

So small and so sleepy, happy
wags from your tail.

I knew when you came home,
together we prevail.

You were playful and

mischievous, energy without end.

We cuddled, took walks, while together we'd mend.

Your generous love, needs, and cuddles.

Dried up my tears, overflowing like puddles.

Grief, anguish, heartache...all too much to bear.

Unless you have a companion with the burden to share.

You are scruffy and lovey, enjoy rubs on the belly.

Oh beautiful, wonderful, pup, we named Ellie.

8. Growth

Like a vine struggling its way up
the side of a decrepit building.
Or a seedling without the
warmth of the sun, the
environment chilling.
The road's without clarity, not
straight, or predictable.
Rather, it's shaped like a paradox,
a secret; invisible.
A mother hawk pushes her Eyas
to flight.
A victim courageously shares her

plight.
Another needs food, clothing,
and shelter.
While a child is buried by their
mother's elder.
Immense and torturous pain
throughout life.
Inescapable and bruising, like the
shriek of a fife.
But through all the trials and
feelings of the loss of control.
There are ways to make meaning,
to surely console.
You reject this belief, with
feelings of loathe.

Too often, this is the way to the thing we call GROWTH.

9. Healing

Dejected and alone, she sits on a cliff.

Not in reality, but I'm painting a glyph.

Degraded and used, with nothing left to give.

She's approached by none other than a devious spiv.

She's expecting the worst, after all she's conditioned.

"Why can't I have peace?"

Feeling imprisoned.

Outrage ensues; enough is
enough; and she uses her voice.
A tone that surprises even her
through the noise.
(She speaks within)
"I am strong, loved and worthy."
(Envelops her inner child, to help
along this journey.)
This child, with tear-stained
cheeks, cries.
"I don't understand, these are all
lies."
The child, through wounds, will
arrive at the healing.
No way to get there unless I love

you, and together, we process the
feeling.

10. Retrograde Poem

What if everything happened in
reverse?
If we began our lives old and
aged the inverse.
Or if we could bend time, and
elongate love cherished.
Could we prevent a catastrophe,
when a loved one had perished?
Would we appreciate life any
more, any less?
Could we feel more confident
expressing love we now

suppress?

I'd like to think that showing love
would be easier.

But as I proclaim my feelings, the
lump in my throat is like a
meteor.

As I age younger the more
curious I am, filled with wonder.

Maybe it would just be
DIFFERENT, with all the same
blunders.

I become smaller and age more
youthful.

Innocence overtakes my voice,
my speech more truthful.

Life is too short, aging forward

or backward; *EITHER WAY.*
As a young toddler now, I gaze
up at my mom, "I love you,"
WITH EASE, I SAY.

11. Unexpected

She was sure of herself,

independent and fierce.

Wounded before, now wearing

armor nothing could pierce.

It was effective at first, but over

time became cumbersome.

A heavy burden to carry,

becoming so troublesome.

Expecting nothing from others,

for that would seem weak.

A take-care-of-yourself attitude,

which to some may sound bleak.

Then by happenstance, meeting a
man not quite like the rest.
There was an energy, a draw, a
spark as you guessed.
Quite unexpected, as this was not
a request.
Too proud and too secretive, she
would never confess.
As she befriends this newfound
stranger,
She is cautious and weary of
danger.
Yet he appeals to her with his
presence of safety.
Her armor is melting, feeling
energy, strangely.

Lighting the way for her future,
as this feeling grows.
It changes everything for her,
and challenges everything she,
"THOUGHT," she, *"KNOWS."*

12. Reincarnation

What if we lived our lives many
times over?
Stumbling to learn lessons like a
secret decoder.
What if we got some things right,
but missed much of the meaning?
Experiencing the feeling of de-ja-
vu as if we were dreaming.
What if the plot played out all
wrong?
We'd certainly need a do-over,
our lessons prolonged.

Whether laughing or crying,
souls intertwined.
Is our destiny predetermined, or
completely undefined?
What if, with loved ones, we will
ALWAYS CONNECT?
So crucial, and vital, that our
lives intersect.
For the intention is to transform
to your highest essence.
Their character as ingredients
leads us to quintessence.
Beyond comprehension is our
next physical form.
Driven by traditional beliefs,
seen as a pseudo-norm.

Maybe we return as different beings altogether.

To illuminate wisdom as a countermeasure.

In one life a man, in another, a dragon.

Maybe one driven by ego, and another with passion.

Endless possibilities are what I envision.

Will you be open to explore this position?

Or will you be suspicious from past conviction?

Afterall, we have free will, it is ultimately *YOUR DECISION.*

OR IS IT?

13. The Knowing

"What," You may ask, "Is THE
KNOWING?"
Poetic dexterity may help the
decoding.
Some may say, "To teach is to
know."
Others use their subconscious as
so.
"The Knowing," to me, has
different dimensions.
An abstract concept of various
conventions.

Maybe it's the confidence you
impersonate.
When writing poetry, juxtaposed
words interpolate.
Or when you tap into the
unconscious world thinking.
And remember your intuition as
if it's God winking.
Or maybe it's that gut-feeling,
INTENSIFIED.
Like a mouse looking at a trap
with cheese and insecticide.
When something is alluring, yet
there's hesitation.
This feeling, "The Knowing," has
a distinct designation.

Whatever you may believe, it is there for a reason.
Maybe a spiritual message, *The Knowing, A Beacon.*

14. Funny Moments

Does anyone else ever think
about their embarrassing times?
Like trying to hide gum from
your home-ec teacher,
Only playing with it in your
hands till it looks like slime.
Putting the whoopie cushion on
the 4th grade teacher's chair.
Only to find later that she
returned the favor, I swear.
Or going to the gym for your
first Zumba class,

Only to realize after, your pants
were reversed on your ass.
Or the time you made that stupid
comment,
I wish I knew the phrase and the
content.
Humiliating at that life stage,
Now, kind of a funny memory, I
gauge.

15. New Year's EVE Party 2025

OUTGOING opened the door to
the party,
and in walked FEAR, just a little
tardy.
They sat down by SHY, who
covered their face with a hat.
COURAGE noticed this and
walked over to chat.
FEAR was intimidated at first
glance.
But PATIENCE arrived, just by

chance.

FEAR nervously looked down at the floor.

So, COURAGE took FEAR's hand, saying no more.

Now FEAR, COURAGE, and PATIENCE were hitting it off,

When along came CONTRADICTION who rolled their eyes with scoff.

WISDOM chimed in, "I love the diversity."

Out of nowhere came PARADOX showing acerbity.

CONTRADICTION knew PARADOX so they ran to greet,

Everyone noticed......adorning them.....AWE SWEEEEET!

SECRET was standing by the punch bowl with MYSTERY; with intense discretion.

When INTERRUPTION fell through the ceiling, making quite an impression!

LESS was a little rushed and forgot to bring a dish to pass.

So, MORE was happy to share, with all their character and class!

SHY gradually came out to mingle,

Then LONELY accidentally bumped COMPANION,

Who...... stated by, OBVIOUS, "Is
no longer single."

16. Letter to Future Me

I am writing a letter to future me.
Feels pretty weird to do
something so free.
I used to feel trapped, chains on
my wrists.
Feeling helpless and hopeless,
but here come some twists.
While now helpful and hopeful, I
am still grieving the living.
But now, with intention and
purpose, I DECIDE to be
GIVING.

Why let torture and anguish turn
my heart to stone?
I have aspirations and goals, yet
to be grown.
Do I dare tell you the future I
envision?
While fate, destiny, or chance
hijack; collision.
Can I please tell you what I want
in conclusion?
When, from the past, I know, it's
all an illusion.
Please hear me out, as I make a
request.
I promise to grow into myself,
with only me to impress.

As I do this with genuine amour,
and intention.
I ask that you guide me with
love, in my reflection.

17. EXPOSED

Exposed, one word, with so
many interpretations.
One showing openness, visibility,
and illumination.
Creating lovers, more intimate,
moreso flawless.
For them, it's the beauty of this
rawness.
Another meaning, the need for
protection from the elements.
Maybe from the brash snap of
winter, like the skin upon

elephants.

Maybe it's that flash of light
that's ruined a precious
photograph from years past.
While another, uses a photo as
blackmail, framed as something it
isn't...pureness to blast.
It's also vulnerability and
strength revealed.
However, when used against
someone, prompts a feeling to be
concealed.
Unmasked and unveiled, such a
wonderous thing.
Yet, unshielded and naked, create
feelings of shame that cling.

Out in the open, bare, or
unprotected.
With or without shelter,
undefended.
An unbelievable word, with so
much to explore.
EXPOSED you are, to richness of
words, more than before.

18. The Plane

You didn't know it, but that was
the exact moment I needed you.
Well, maybe not *YOU*, but you
were someone I already knew!
It was at that time I had lost
much of my hope.
Talking to you that night made it
easier for me to cope.

You see, it wasn't that I wasn't in
a good place.

But more that I was in a little
heartbroken space.
And through conversation, I
found that you were too.
Was fate pushing us together,
was this our cue?
You shared a little of your life
with me, maybe just a glimpse.
While I too, offered a piece of my
past, though I'm more of a wimp.
We continued to share stories,
feelings, times of hope and of
pain.
Our friendship, it started, I guess,
that night, on that plane.
Or...maybe before, when we

worked together.
That was a shitshow some days,
quite an adventure.
With few interactions, I still saw
who you were.
Kind and intelligent, though you
remembered it blurred.
Then I asked you to accompany
me to a show.
I had a great time, hilariously
awkward though.
We bonded over days at the gym,
building our muscles.
You, training for weightlifting,
me overcoming my mental
puzzles.

Who knows why our paths cross,
but I could guess that it's for life
to take a necessary pause, or
maybe even to share the pain of
loss.
But when we come together in
life as a friend, we tend to blend
our lives, which I highly
recommend!
Ok, logging off as this plane is
about to descend.

19. UNBROKEN

So, I've experienced my fair share
of trials and tribulations.
While getting to this point in my
life, at forty-five, I shudder with
lamentation.
For many things, I'm thankful
for, such as a safe, and loving
youth.
But as time lapsed into
adulthood, I noticed my decisions
which lacked couth.
Palpably, I started to see the

cracks in my decisions.

The life I created, walls closing
in, more and more restrictions.
Until I could no longer stand or
remember who I was.
My identity was shattered, from
gaslighting, a type of toxic scuzz.
A battle waged within; pressure
creating more creases.
Until I hit my breaking point,
fragments exploded into pieces.
But as I realize now, maybe that
was the way to become whole.
Maybe the only way to find
yourself again is to rediscover
your soul.

Maybe every choice we make is
actually the path leading home.
Turbulent, winding, and twisted,
leading ultimately to *Shalom*.
There were many points on this
journey where I felt weak, words
unspoken.
But I am stronger now,
undeniably, forever and ever,
UNBROKEN.

20. Racoon

It was the beginning of Mercury
Retrograde.
Let me paint the scene, get ready
for an escapade.
My friend, she works a job at a
yard, well underpaid.
When, one morning, arriving at
work, suddenly attacked, and
afraid.
She had reached down, to coil up
a hose, likely decayed.
And out of nowhere sprang a

racoon, like an unclipped
grenade.
Yelling for help, calling her
family, everyone was dismayed.
Now, off to the hospital, she must
masquerade.
Now getting a series of rabies
shots, so germs don't invade.
Her phone rings, her boss
demands a drug test, she is
shocked and feeling betrayed.
"Do drugs make racoons attack?"
Her boss remains un-swayed.
Anger and resentment bubble up
now, after working there over a
decade.

"I got the rabies shots and the drug test," the message relayed. She's wishing she could fry that racoon, or maybe her boss, sauteed. Or maybe even get revenge, (going too far...) or...strangulate. Luckily, she is ultimately ok, Stephanie...one to commemorate.

21. The Poetry Contest

Writing poems can be

exceptionally grand.

Unless you procrastinate, like me,

ideas unplanned.

I took the first step and entered

the contest festivity.

My creativity poured out, with

genuine authenticity.

With 21 poems to write in 21

days,

You know I waited until five days

left, my mind in a haze.

So, there I just started, putting
pen to the paper.
When I told my friends, I'm
guessing they wagered.
On if all of the poems I would
actually finish by deadline.
Or if I'd be calling and crying to
them on their friend hotline.
I thank my friends for the
inspiration to do this, I am
grateful.
I hope you all like some of my
poetry and find that it's tasteful!
Well, here it is, this is it, the
finish line.

Happy New Year's Eve, let's go
have a glass of red wine!

9 789369 542062